Eve Blossom Has Wheels

German literature is well known for its rich love poetry of all varieties and moods. More than any other, it has inspired settings by the most famous composers. For this reason, some of the great love poetry by Goethe, Mörike, Heine and others is familiar to music lovers throughout the world. However, it is hardly known outside the concert hall. This selection sets out to repair this gap for the English-speaking world. It contains a choice of German (also some Austrian and Swiss) love poetry from the Minnesänger of the Middle Ages, through the little-known but abundant period of German Baroque and the Romanticism of the late eighteenth and early nineteenth centuries, down to the modern voices of the twentieth century.

The mood of the poetry inevitably changes over the nearly thousand-year span of this collection, but what is often more striking is the variety of mood found within each period – satire among the Minnesänger, humour and even burlesque among the Romantics, and romanticism among the modernists.

KEITH BOSLEY is a poet and translator. He translated *The Kalevala* for Oxford World's Classics and was awarded the English Goethe Society's prize for his translations of Goethe.

Eve Blossom Has Wheels

German Love Poetry

SELECTED AND TRANSLATED BY

Keith Bosley

LIBRIS

This collection first published 1997

Translation copyright © Keith Bosley 1997

Kurt Schwitters's 'Eve Blossom Has Wheels' in this version © the Themerson Archive, 1996

All rights reserved

Libris
10 Burghley Road
London NW5 1UE

A catalogue record for this book is available from the British Library

ISBN 1 870352 52 1

ACKNOWLEDGEMENTS

We would like to thank the following for their kind permission to use material under their copyright: Luchterhand Literaturverlag for Ernst Jandl's 'pain through friction'; Atrium Verlag for Erich Kästner's 'Ode to Joy' and for Erich Ohser's drawing which originally accompanied it; the Estate of Mascha Kaléko for 'Pihi'; and the Estate of Kurt Schwitters and the Themerson Archive for 'Eve Blossom Has Wheels' (first published in Stefan Themerson's *Kurt Schwitters in England, 1940–1948*, Gaberbocchus Press, London, 1958).

Designed and produced by Kitzinger, London
Printed and bound by Biddles Ltd, Guildford

CONTENTS

	Page
Anonymous (12th century)	
'You're for me, I'm for you'	11
'Were the whole world mine'	11
'Floret silva undique'	11
from *The Song of the Nibelungs*	
Siegfried meets Kriemhild	12
Der von Kürenberc (12th century)	
The Falcon	14
Henric van Veldeke (12th century)	
Tristan and I	15
True Love	16
Heinrich von Morungen (?–1222)	
The Lover	17
As Day was Dawning	18
Wolfram von Eschenbach (13th century)	
Day the Dragon	20
Walther von der Vogelweide (*c.* 1170–1230)	
'Under the lime tree'	22
'Deep in a melancholy mood'	23
Gottfried von Strassburg (13th century)	
from *Tristan*	
The Noble heart	24
Lamer	25
Traditional	
Ballad of the Royal Children	27
Georg Rudolf Weckherlin (1584–1653)	
Love is Life and Death	29

Martin Opitz (1597–1639)
    To his Coy Mistress   30
    The Platonick Lover   31

Paul Fleming (1609–40)
    How He Would Like to be Kissed   32

Andreas Gryphius (1616–64)
    To Eugenia, Who Bade Him Burn Her Letter   33

Christian Hofmann von Hofmannswaldau (1617–79)
    On the Mouth   34
    He Watches Lesbia Through a Hole   34

Philipp von Zesen (1619–89)
    On the Eyes of his Love   35

Gottlieb Stolle (1673–1744)
    Love's Metamorphosis   36

Johann Christian Günther (1695–1723)
    On Giving Phyllis a Ring with a Death's Head   37
    A Splendid Pair   38
    Love Spurn'd   38

Johann Wilhelm Ludwig Gleim (1719–1803)
    Gather ye Rosebuds   40

Johann Wolfgang von Goethe (1749–1832)
    Wedding Night   41
    Welcome and Parting   42
    The Violet   43
    from *Faust*
        Gretchen at the spinning-wheel, alone   44
    Lili's Park   45
    To Charlotte von Stein   50
    A Song of Mignon   52
    Amor as Landscape Painter   52

The Fifth Roman Elegy	55
Nearness of her Beloved	56
from *West-Eastern Divan*	
Blessed Longing	56
'Luxuriant on branches'	57
Ginkgo biloba	58

Marianne von Willemer (1784–1860)
from Goethe's *West-Eastern Divan*
  'What's the meaning of this motion?' — 59
Memorial — 60

Friedrich Hölderlin (1770–1843)
  Applause of Men — 61
  Home — 61
  Socrates and Alcibiades — 62
  The Parting — 62

Clemens Brentano (1778–1842)
  Spinner's Song — 64

Des Knaben Wunderhorn (1805–8)
  'My father told me' — 65

Adelbert von Chamisso (1781–1838)
from *Woman's Love and Life*
  'He, most glorious of mortals' — 66

Joseph von Eichendorff (1788–1857)
  Formerly — 67

Wilhelm Müller (1794–1827)
  Impatience — 68

August von Platen (1796–1835)
  Ghazal — 69

Annette von Droste-Hülshoff (1797–1848)
  Young Love — 70

Heinrich Heine (1797–1856)
   from *The Book of Songs*
      'From my great woes'   72
      'A fellow loves a girl'   72
      'They sat drinking tea'   73
      'I do not know the meaning'   74
      'Silent the night'   75
      'You are like a flower'   75

Eduard Mörike (1804–75)
   A Girl's First Love Song   76
   The Forsaken Maid   77
   Fair Rohtraut   77
   Domestic Scene   79

Theodor Storm (1817–88)
   Hyacinths   83
   'In words you do not want to say it'   83
   A Lesson   84

Klaus Groth (1819–99)
   Where there's a will   85

Conrad Ferdinand Meyer (1825–98)
   Lethe   86

Richard Dehmel (1863–1920)
   from *Two People*
      'Two people are walking through a bare, cold grove'   88

Stefan George (1868–1933)
   from *The Book of the Hanging Gardens*
      'If I do not touch you today'   90
   from *The New Realm*
      'You pure and slender as a flame'   90

Christian Morgenstern (1871–1914)
   Bim Bam Bong   92
   The Two Parallels   93

Hugo von Hofmannsthal (1874–1929)
   The Two of Them   94

Rainer Maria Rilke (1875–1926)
   Love Song   95
   Leda   95

Georg Heym (1887–1912)
   'Your eyelashes, so long'   97

Kurt Schwitters (1887–1948)
   Eve Blossom has Wheels   99

Erich Kästner (1899–1974)
   Ode to Joy   101

Mascha Kaléko (1907–75)
   Pihi   102

Ernst Jandl (1925–)
   pain through friction   103

Notes   104

Index of Poets   112

FOR SATU

The poetry known as German (the name includes
the Austrians and some Swiss and a scattered few)
    proceeds like so much else in those parts
    fitfully – rather, by Golden Ages.

The first was that of Wolfram von Eschenbach
and those who learnt their craft from the Troubadours –
    great Minnesingers bringing courtly
    love with its delicate tones and rhythms.

The second age was Luther's, or what he left –
Renaissance sacrificed for a single tongue:
    Baroque explored in new directions
    just as astronomers probed for planets.

The third was Goethe's age – it was Schubert's too:
Romantic love, and nature in all her moods
    songs sung by peasants named a homeland
    Classical metres were scanned anew – thus.

Was there a fourth age? Some of us think it came
with Rilke, alienation and irony
    and went with Hitler: Brecht besought us
    not to remember it too severely.

But our presiding genius is the god
of love that now is mutual, now is not,
    now blest, now damned by circumstances,
    mostly respectable, not so sometimes.

This book of borrowed voices is yours, *mein Schatz*,
to say in print some things that I need to say
    until such time as you will let me
    publish the verses which only we know.

                                              K. B.

Anonymous

You're for me, I'm for you:
never doubt that is true.
You are locked within
my heart and my skin
and no one will find the key:
there for ever you must be.

Were the whole world mine
from the ocean to the Rhine
I would go without its charms
if the queen of England were
lying in my arms.

Floret silva undique:
woe is me when he's away.
Green the woods on every side:
where does he so long abide?
He has ridden off:
alas, who shall be my love?

SIEGFRIED MEETS KRIEMHILD

    Lord Siegfried was delighted
      and merry was his thought
    for in his heart he carried
      a joy quite unfraught
    that he would soon be meeting
      the fair Ute's child
    and her way of greeting
      was duly sweet and mild.

    When she saw before her
      the man with high-held head
    his cheeks flushing scarlet
      then the fair maid said:
    'Lord Siegfried, you are welcome,
      excellent noble knight!'
    His spirits at that greeting
      rose to a greater height.

    He bowed low in devotion
      but she took his hand:
    how sweet beside the lady
      it was for him to stand!
    The lord and — yes — the lady
      cast a loving eye
    towards one another
      but they did so secretly.

Did white hands press together
 tenderly to show
their hearts' great passion?
 Well, I do not know
but I cannot imagine
 that nothing took place
for she betrayed her feelings
 soon enough in her face.

Neither the summer season
 nor the month of May
could have made him happy
 as his heart was that day —
so great and high his joy was
 that he felt there and then
as hand in hand he wandered
 with her he hoped to win.

from The Song of the Nibelungs *(stanzas 291–5)*

Der von Kürenberc

THE FALCON

    I raised me a falcon
        for more than a year.
    When I had tamed and trained it
        after my desire
    and when all its feathers
        with gold I had well bound
    it soared high above me
        and flew to another land.

    Since then I have seen the falcon
        in handsome flight:
    it was wearing silken jesses
        upon its feet
    and as for its feathers
        they were red gold.
    May God bring them together
        who are in love and long to hold!

Henric van Veldeke

TRISTAN AND I

    Undeniable emotion
    Tristan to Isolde drove
    all because he drank a potion
    not because he was in love.
    Good my lady, my devotion
    passes his: I have a notion
    it is me you ought to thank
    that I love who never drank.
      Well-endowed one
      far too proud one
      come to bed
      with me instead!

TRUE LOVE

In the season of the year
when the days are growing long
and the skies again are clear
then the blackbirds make good cheer
publishing afresh their song
with its tidings glad and dear:
then to God all thanks belong
   who has sent true love
and no man can prove him wrong.

I am glad because of her
who to me such good has done
that I turn from all my care
which long held me in despair.
This is how my fate has gone:
I am rich beyond compare
since I lost all I had won
   and she gave true love
with no doubts to brood upon.

Though my great good luck annoys
those who hate to see me so
I can suffer it with poise
for I would not dodge my joys:
that is why I will not go
after those whose gloom destroys
since her kindly look I know
   who for her true love
lets me languish in my woe.

Heinrich von Morungen

THE LOVER

I heard on the lea
a loud voice and a sweet air:
I was equally
rich with joy, sick with despair.
I discovered her
whom to cheer
was my care
dancing as she sang with voice so clear:
merrily
I ran there.

I found her, a furrow
on her brow, alone, cheeks wet
that day on whose morrow
she thought I had met my fate:
but her very hate
higher I rate
than of late
when I knelt before her as she sat
and her sorrow
quite forgat.

I found her alone
on the ramparts – I'd been called:
she'd have been my own –
nor did I need to be bold.
My fire might have swirled

through the world
unforetold
if her sweet love's bonds had not laid hold
and brought down
sense blindfold.

AS DAY WAS DAWNING

'Alas, but when again for me
 will her fine body, white
 as any snow can be
 shed lustre through the night?
 My eyes mistook its gleam:
 to me it could but seem
 a glittering moonbeam
   as day was dawning.'

'Alas, but when again will he
 tarry here till the morrow?
 So that as night fades we
 will no more need to sorrow:
 Alas, now it is day
 I heard him sadly say
 when last with me he lay
   as day was dawning.'

'Alas, she kissed me as I slept –
 I could not keep the toll,
 and many tears she wept –
 down, down I saw them roll:
 I soothed her, wiped her face

> until in sorrow's place
> there was a wild embrace
>   as day was dawning.'

'Alas, so often he has pressed me –
  his thirst, I could not slake it.
He wished when he undressed me
to see my poor self naked
with nothing that could stifle.
I count it no mere trifle:
he never missed his eyeful
  as day was dawning!'

Wolfram von Eschenbach

DAY THE DRAGON

     'Its claw
has ripped the clouds apart,
it rises with great might:
   I saw
day the grey dragon start —
day that will turn the knight
I let in with such care
from his sweet company.
I'll see him out: I dare
do this for one of quality.'

   'You sing,
watchman, a song that checks
my joy and swells my sorrow:
   you bring
such news to me as breaks
my heart against each morrow.
Keep it from me, good man,
I order you, refrain:
I'll pay you what I can
for my companion to remain.'

   'My sweet
lady, he must be gone
forthwith: give him your leave.
   Discreet
his love be from now on,

       his fame and life to save.
       To see him out again
       was a task in my trust.
       It is day: 'twas night when
    I gave him to your lips and breast.'

         'Your choice
       your song be, watchman: here
       leave love's provider, taster.
         Your voice
       filled him and me with fear
       even before the daystar
       rose on the one who came
       for love, or light could dart:
       you often took him from
    my white arms, never from my heart.'

         Because
       the glass was bright with day
       the watchman sang his warning:
            she was
       afraid for him who lay
       and breasts to breast that morning
       she pressed. Despite the song
       the knight did not forget
       his courage: long and long,
    kisses and much else paid love's debt.

Walther von der Vogelweide

'Under the lime tree
on the heath
where the bed of us two was
   there you may see
   sweetly both
broken flowers and broken grass.
By the forest in a dale –
   tandaraday! –
sweetly sang the nightingale.

I made my way
to the meadow
where my lover had come before:
   he welcomed me
   with Noble Lady
and I am happy evermore.
Did he kiss me? Ooh, and how –
   tandaraday!
See how red my mouth is now.

There with craft
he had laid out
with flowers such a lovely bed.
   They will have laughed
   but not aloud
who along that path may tread.
From the roses well they may –

    tandaraday! –
mark the spot where my head lay.

    Should it be known
    he lay with me
(God forbid!) I'd be ashamed.
    What we alone
    did secretly
let it nevermore be named
but by us or by the bird –
    tandaraday! –
who will not tell what we shared!'

    Deep in a melancholy mood
    there I was sitting and was thinking
    that I would leave her servitude
    when a hope kept my thoughts from sinking.
A hope – not really: that is setting it too high!
  Then a small hopelet: still too big by half –
So small that, if I ever tell you, you will laugh.
But nobody is glad if he does not know why.

    A stalk of grass has made me glad:
    it says I'll benefit from staying.
    I measured off that little blade
    as I've seen children do when playing.
Now listen and take note of what the bits foretell:
  'She will, she won't, she will, she won't, she will.'
However many times I did it, it worked still.
That gives me hope, but faith must play its part as well.

Gottfried von Strassburg

THE NOBLE HEART

There is a common argument
to which I largely assent:
the love-sick spirit, the more is
its dealing with love stories
the more is its suffering.
I would stand by this, but one thing
takes its stand against me:
whoever is in love deeply
though it puts his heart in pain
that heart gladly takes the strain.
The spirit full of desire
the more it flames in love's fire
and the more its passions roar
so its love will burn the more.
This grief is so full of joy
this ill sets the heart so high
that no noble heart will fly it
having once been heartened by it.
This as sure as death I know
and have learnt from the same woe:
the noble lover glories
(mark my words!) in love stories.
Hence who longs for a tale of love
has travelled far enough.
I will tell him a story
of noble lovers whose glory
was pure love perfectly proved:
a lover and his beloved;
a man – a woman, a woman – a man;
Tristan – Isolde, Isolde – Tristan.

(lines 101–130)

She propped herself and leaned
against him with her elbow:
their boldness began so.
Her mirror-bright eyes
filled with miseries:
her heart began to well,
her sweet mouth to swell,
her head drooped right down.
Her friend thereupon began
to take her in an embrace,
not too aloof nor too close,
but as he would treat a guest.

His speech was of the gentlest:
'Ah, fair sweet one, tell me plain:
what is wrong, why do you complain?'
Isolde, Love's game-bird, sware:
'*Lamer* is all my care,
lamer oppresses my heart,
lamer deals me a great smart.'

When so much of *lamer* she spoke
he considered, undertook
to mine all meanings that stirred
in the depths of that word.
He recalled soon enough
that *l'amer* was love,
l'amer bitter, *la mer* the sea:
its meanings seemed an army.
He let that third meaning go
and asked about these two:
of love nothing he quoth

that was mistress of them both,
the hope, the desire they shared.

Of sea and bitter he declared:
'I believe, Isolde fair,
sea and bitter are your care:
waves and wind have battered you.
You are embittered by these two.'
'No, my lord, no! What are you saying?
Neither do I find dismaying.
I can bear both wind and sea:
lamer alone hurts me.'

When he sounded out the word
and love deep within it heard
he said in an undertone:
'Fair one, such thoughts are my own:
lamer and you, you are my care.
Wife of my heart, Isolde dear,
you alone and your love
have twisted my senses off
and taken them clean away:
I have gone astray
so far and so sore
I shall find myself nevermore.
I am troubled and oppressed,
I am shamed and distressed
by all that my eyes behold:
there is nothing in all the world
in my heart so dear as you.'
She said: 'My lord, I feel this too.'

from Tristan *(lines 11970–12028)*

Traditional

BALLAD OF THE
ROYAL CHILDREN

There were two royal children
Who loved each other so much
But far too deep was the water
And they could never touch.

If you can swim, O sweetheart
Then swim across to me
And I will light three candles
And they will show you the way.

A faithless nun she heard that
Pretending to be asleep
And she put out the candles
And the young man drowned so deep.

O fisherman, dear fisher
A reward to you I'll bring
If you sink your nets in the water
And fish me the son of a king!

Into her arms she took him
And on his red mouth she fell:
O mouth, were you but speaking
My young heart would be well.

She wrapped her cloak about her
And leapt right into the sea:
Goodnight, my father and mother
No more will you see me!

And then the bells began tolling
And in grief and woe 'twas said:
Here lie two royal children
And both of them are dead.

LOVE IS LIFE AND DEATH

This life I lead is kin to very death
And more than death itself my cheerless life;
Death is the end of human pain and life
But my life knows no ending by this death.

Something I see can injure me to death
And something else can bring me back to life
Till by a glance I am dealt now death, now life,
And in an hour I learn both life and death.

Ah, love! Grant me henceforth another life –
If I am to live – or else another death
For I love neither this death nor this life.

Forgive me, love, I am yours in life and death
And death with you is exquisite sweet life
And life when far from you most bitter death.

Martin Opitz

TO HIS COY MISTRESS

Ah, dearest, let us hurry,
    We still have time:
For both of us to tarry
    Would be a crime.
The gifts of fairest beauty
    Flee step by step,
Everything that we have must
    Sink to the deep.
Your fine cheeks will grow pallid,
    And grey your hair,
Your bright eyes will turn rheumy,
    To ice their flare;
Your coral mouth on splendour
    Will lose its hold,
Your snow-white hands will tremble
    And you'll grow old.
So let us make the most of
    The fruits of youth,
Before we have to face the
    Moment of truth.
While to yourself you're loving
    Then love me true,
Give me what, when you give it,
    I shall lose too.

THE PLATONICK LOVER

Would that this half of me which we call physical
This meanest part of me I might consume with fire
Might like Alcmene's son whose courage could not tire
Burn off my burden here, this body that is vile

To go to heaven! My spirit begins to hasten hence
Towards something better, but this flesh, this handful of blood
Must undergo exchange for some far better good
Unknown to mortal flesh and blood and common sense.

My light, set me ablaze with your eyes brightly burning
That from this skin, this body's gloomy vapour turning
This dungeon full of chaos and dread I may take wing

And unencumbered, loose and from all weakness freed
Far above every air and heaven I may spend
To gaze upon that Beauty whence your beauties spring!

Paul Fleming

HOW HE WOULD LIKE TO BE KISSED

Nowhere else but on the lips:
Then it sinks to the heart's deeps.
Not too ready, not too wrung,
Nor with a reluctant tongue.

Not too little, not too much:
That is children playing touch.
Not too loud and not too soft:
Moderation hold aloft!

Not too far and not too near:
That brings yearning, this brings care.
Not too dry and not too wet,
As Adonis Venus met.

Not too cold and not too hot,
Now together and now not;
Not too fast and not too slow,
Not forgetting where to go.

Half with breath and half with teeth,
With the lips dipped half beneath;
Not forgetting when to be –
Better two than company.

Kiss now, every girl and man
As you know, will, shall and can!
Only I know, and my Miss,
What is the right way to kiss.

Andreas Gryphius

TO EUGENIA, WHO BADE HIM BURN HER LETTER

Just as a wayfarer who, when the gloomy night
With its thick darkness cloaks the air, the land, the sea,
Gloomily roams this way and that, and fearfully
Does not know where to go nor what to do aright,

Just so it is with me; yet when the moon awakes
And lights her beaming candle in the house of cloud,
He soon finds way and bearing: so my spirit is bowed
No more, and from your letter's smile new comfort takes.

And yet why do you bid me burn this lovely sign?
To recognise amid my night the flames as mine?
This fire within my heart will show you who I am.

O fairest, should this paper merely touch my breast,
Forthwith in ashes then it will be quite laid waste
Unless my weeping grants it freedom from the flame.

Christian Hofmann von Hofmannswaldau

ON THE MOUTH

Mouth! that can drive two souls to clutch each other tight
Mouth! so much sweeter than the strongest wine of heaven
Mouth! where the alicant of life is poured and given
Mouth! I would rather have than Jewish wealth and might
Mouth! whose strong balm can either fortify or smite
Mouth! to outblush whose joy the rose has vainly striven
Mouth! with which not a ruby ever can draw even
Mouth! which the Graces' fountains moisten and make bright
Mouth! oh of coral hue, mouth my unique delight
Mouth! on your purple let one kiss from me alight!

HE WATCHES LESBIA THROUGH A HOLE

Lesbia thought that she was quite alone
As she secured the windows and the doors,
But Sylvius chose to flout all decent laws
And through a hole he looked where she had gone.

On her left knee she laid her leg – the right,
Her hand was busy fastening her shoe,
He saw the moss her scarlet part shone through,
Where Cupid seeks his cradle with delight.

Sylvius cried: How elegant that thigh
Decked in warm snow, inlaid with ivory!
He saw the place his hopes could not abandon.

Sylvius laughed. She said: Your passion's spent!
The pain is yours, mine the embarrassment
For now your hopes have not a leg to stand on.

ON THE EYES OF HIS LOVE

Her eyes so full of flames! What flames? No, garnet rays:
Again no! They are lightnings flashing through the air
That travel from her eyes until they meet my stare.
Not lightnings: bolts with which she wontedly displays,

With which she wontedly in coin love's tribute pays.
Not bolts, but suns they are, with which she busily tries
To dazzle others' light, which reaches no one's eyes
For fear of punishment. No sun, no starlight plays

From her brow's heaven: still no! From all that I see shimmer,
No flames burn so, such rays no garnet ever had,
Lightning has no such power, no arrow can make glad,
The sun is not so strong, a star cannot so glimmer:

So why are they seen by folk whose wits have strayed too far
As flames, as garnet, lightning, arrow, sun and star?

Gottlieb Stolle

LOVE'S
METAMORPHOSIS

Amor, you have transformed me first into a deer
That bears its hunter's arrow in its tender breast;
Thereafter into a swan that sings before it dies,
And then into a flower the sun's rays cauterise,
Flaming upon its sap until its bloom is sere,
Whereupon I dissolved into a tearful rain;
Now must I in my agony
A salamander be
That in the fiery beams which Daphne's eyes contain
Languishes, yet meanwhile to its longing heart give cheer.

Anyway I'd not want to grumble in the least
If but your wondrous might
That hitherto for me planned no delight
Should at long last grant me your favour
And ere I die transform me into Daphne's lover.

Johann Christian Günther

ON GIVING PHYLLIS
A RING WITH
A DEATH'S HEAD

> At this love-token take no fright:
> Our future likeness it portrays
> And only turns their faces white
> Who set at nothing reason's ways.
> Yet how can ice be paired with flame?
> Can love and death resound the same?
> These pairs resound with equal worth
> Only too well, for both have power
> Their several miracles to shower
> On everyone who walks the earth.
>
> I give this pledge to teach you thus:
> The gold means firm fidelity,
> The ring, that time may favour us,
> The dove, how happy we may be,
> The head, that life in thought may reign;
> In the grave every wish is vain,
> So love and live while still you can,
> Who knows how soon we must dismiss!
> Life lives most in a faithful kiss:
> It is high time our time began!

A SPLENDID PAIR

Was ever such a splendid pair?
Who else could call such joys their own –
Her laughing mouth, her flying hair,
Her full breasts bouncing up and down?
Yearning abhors a vacuum,
I do not know what I desire.
Our human life is called a dream:
Would such a dream my own life were!

LOVE SPURN'D

I have had enough!
Hot pleasures and kisses
Are poisonous blisses
Not meant to improve:
O come, blessed freedom, and put out the blaze
That turned all my wits and left me in a daze!

But what was I doing?
I see now the source
Of love's crazy force
For I am more knowing:
I shatter my fetters, I set my heart free
And hate with a purpose that fond agony.

What torment have I?
What sorrow encumbers
My everynight slumbers?
The time has passed by,

O jewel most costly! Incalculable loss!
O had I known sooner how fickle she was!

   Go, beauty, be quick!
   Your prettiest looks
   Can catch on sharp hooks:
   I well know your trick.
Her letters in flames and her ring snapt in two
Will show to my fair one that I have come through.

   Yes, through I have come
   And swear from my heart:
   To kiss and to flirt
   Is nonsense and dumb,
For who falls in love is not like to improve,
So go, fickle siren! I have had enough!

Johann Wilhelm Ludwig Gleim

GATHER YE ROSEBUDS

Roses, pluck them as they blow,
   Tomorrow is not today!
Let not even one hour go,
   Time flies on its way!

Drink and kiss! For you must borrow
   Time while yet you may;
Say, where will you be tomorrow?
   Time flies on its way!

He who thinks a chance comes twice
   Lives to rue the day;
Live fast — that is my advice:
   Time flies on its way!

WEDDING NIGHT

Far from the feasting, in the bedroom
Amor sits loyal, his fears increase
Lest wanton guests are planning mischief
To undermine the bride-bed's peace.
Aflame with mystic holy glitter
Pale gold before him is deployed;
A swirl of incense fills the chamber,
By both of you to be enjoyed.

How your heart beats as the hour is striking,
Driving your noisy guests away!
How for the fair mouth you are glowing
That, mute, will let you have your way!
You hurry to the consummation
With her into the sanctuary
And in the watchman's hands the fire burns
Low as a night-light, silently.

How with your overwhelming kisses
Her bosom quakes, and all her beauty!
But now her sternness turns to trembling,
For now your boldness turns to duty.
With Amor's help you quickly undress her
Yet he's not half so quick as you;
Then, roguish and discreet as ever,
Shuts his eyes tightly to the view.

WELCOME AND PARTING

My heart beat fast: to horse, and quickly!
No sooner thought when up I swung.
Evening was lulling the earth already
And night upon the mountains hung.
Already in its misty mantle
The oak, a towering giant, stood there
Where shadows looked out from the thicket
In hundreds with a black-eyed stare.

The moon emerging from a cloud-bank
Gloomy through haze I saw it peer,
The winds on subtle wings were moving,
Dreadfully brushing by my ear;
Though night brought forth a thousand monsters
My courage soared, would not say no,
For in my veins what fire was burning!
And in my heart, oh, what a glow!

I saw you, and the gentle sweetness
Flowed on me from your lovely gaze,
And at your side my heart stood firmly,
My every breath was yours always.
A rosy-tinted vernal weather
Surrounded your delicious face,
And what – ye gods! – I hoped for, never
Deserved from you, a tenderness!

But oh, the morning sun already
Brings parting to constrict my heart,
For in your kisses what a rapture,
But in your eye how great the smart!

I went, you stood there staring downward,
Stared after me with liquid eye;
And yet, what joy to be beloved!
And to love, gods, oh, what a joy!

THE VIOLET

A violet in the meadow grew,
With drooping head and hid from view;
   It was a pretty flower.
Then a young shepherdess came by
With tripping step and sparkling eye
   That way, that way
   Across the meadow singing.

Ah! thinks the violet, would I were
The fairest bloom in nature's store
   For but one little hour,
Till by the darling I was plucked
And firmly in her bosom tucked
   For but, for but
   A moment to her clinging!

Ah, but alas! the girl came there
And of the violet unaware
   Trampled the hapless flower.
It sank and died and yet was glad:
For though I die, my death I had
   From her, from her,
   Her feet so lightly springing.

GRETCHEN AT THE SPINNING-WHEEL, ALONE

My peace is gone,
My heart is sore;
I'll find peace never
And nevermore.

Where he is not
I cannot be,
The whole world has
Gone sour on me.

My wretched head
Is quite confused
And my poor wits
Are broken and bruised.

My peace is gone,
My heart is sore;
I'll find peace never
And nevermore.

Only for him
I look through the glass,
Only to him
Through the door I pass.

His lofty bearing,
His noble guise,
The smile of his mouth,
The power of his eyes,

A magic stream,
That talk of his,
The squeeze of his hand,
And oh, his kiss!

My peace is gone,
My heart is sore;
I'll find peace never
And nevermore.

My bosom hankers
After him:
Oh, might I grasp
Him, cling to him

And kiss him
As much as I may
And on his kisses
Slip away!

from Faust

LILI'S PARK

But no menagerie exists
As motley as my Lili's show!
In it she has the most amazing beasts
And gets them in, she knows not how.
Oh how they leap and run and patter,
And though their wings are clipped they flutter –
The wretched princes all at once
Whom an undying love torments!

'Who was the witch? – Lili?' – Say not a word!
If you don't know her, well then, thank the Lord.

Oh, what a clamour, what a cackling
When at the gate she takes her stand
And holds the feeding basket in her hand!
Oh, what a squeaking, what a quacking!
Every tree, every bush
Seems to spring to life, and whole
Multitudes fall
At her feet; in the pool the very fish
Impatiently splash, push their heads out.
And she strews the feed about
With a look fit to delight gods,
Let alone the brutes. Then each head nods
As it pokes, sips and pecks;
They fall on one another's necks,
They shove, they throng, they fight,
They hound, they scare, they bite,
And all for a scrap of bread
That, though dry, from the lovely hands that gripped it
Tastes as if she in ambrosia had dipped it.

But still her look! her tone
When she calls: Pipi! Pipi!
Would draw Jupiter's eagle from his throne,
And Venus' pair of doves,
Even the peacock nothing moves
I swear would come this way
If they but heard her voice from far away.
For from the forest's gloom she has brought
A bear, unlicked and quite untrained,
In her custody to be restrained,
In her tame company to be taught
To do with the others as he ought:
Up to a certain point, of course!

How fair, and oh! how good
She seemed! I would have shed my blood
To feed her flowerbed.

'You say: *me*! How? Who? Where?'
Very well, gentlemen: *I* am the bear,
Caught in a net about my ass,
At her feet on a silken thread.
But how it all came to pass
Another time I'll say:
I'm too angry today.

For look! now cornered here I sit
And hear from far away the chattering,
And see the flittering, the fluttering,
I turn around
And growl,
And double backward for a bit
And look around
And growl,
And run on forward for a bit,
And for a last time turn around.

Then suddenly the raging starts,
A mighty spirit sniffs and snorts,
The inner nature begins to fret.
What, you a mere fool, a leveret!
Pipi indeed! A squirrel, nuts you'll crack!
I ruffle up my bristly neck,
I am not used to serve.
Every tree trimmed so neatly has the nerve
To scorn me! I flee the enameld green,
The grass mown oh so evenly;
The box tree cocks a snook at me,

I flee to the darkest bush and hide within,
To push through the hedge and hence
To leap over the fence!
But climbing, leaping are denied me,
A spell is weighing me down,
A spell would have me drown,
I wearily toil, but toils have tied me,
Then I collapse in cataracts made by man
And champ and weep and roll about half dead,
But ah! I cannot hope for aid
From Oreads of porcelain.

Suddenly! Ah, a fair,
A blessed feeling courses through my every member!
'Tis she, who is singing in her arbour there!
I hear the dear, dear voice I well remember,
And the whole air is full of warm spring smells.
Oh, does she sing for me to hear her trills?
I press that way, trampling shrubs where I clamber,
For me the bushes part, the trees retreat,
And so – the beast is lying at her feet.

She looks at it: 'A monster! How amusing!
For a bear too mild,
For a poodle too wild;
So shaggy, rough, coarse – not my choosing!'
Her little foot strokes him along his back;
He thinks he is in paradise.
How all his seven senses quake!
And she – looks on as cool as ice.
I kiss her shoe, chew on the sole,
So nicely, as none but a bear may;
Quite gently I get up and stealthily I crawl
Soft at her knee . . . On the right day

She lets it happen, scratches me round the ear
And pats me hard, but in a wanton way,
And newly born to bliss, I purr.
Then sweetly, idly mocking she calls out:
'*Allons tout doux! eh la menotte!*
Et faites Serviteur,
Comme un joli Seigneur.'
Such is her style, with jest and wit!
Hope spurs the fool, so often cheated;
But let him push his luck a little bit
And her tight rein will be repeated.

But she has too a flask of jungle-juice
That like no earthly honey drips,
From which, and just once, with her fingertips
She smears, tempered with love and tenderness,
A drop upon her monster's thirsting lips
And once again flees and abandons me,
And then I am unbound and free
Yet tethered, always drawn to her,
I seek her, shrink, and flee once more.
She lets the blighted wretch stray, not too far:
It is his pleasure, is his silent woe;
Ha! many times she leaves my door ajar,
Watching me mockingly, though I've no wish to go.

As for me! – gods, it is in your hands
Whether this stifling magic ends:
I'll thank you if you set me free at length!
But if from you no kind assistance comes,
Not quite in vain do I thus flex my limbs:
I feel! I swear! I still have strength.

TO CHARLOTTE VON STEIN

Wherefore did you give us these deep glimpses
Of our future so we need not guess
Nor entrust ourselves in sweet delusion
To our love, our earthly happiness?
Wherefore did you give us, Fate, these feelings
So to look into each other's heart
And to set amid these strange confusions
How we really are upon a chart?

Oh, so many thousand people hardly
Know their own hearts, drifting senselessly,
Floating aimless back and forth and hopeless
Swirl in torment they did not foresee;
Then rejoice again when they behold the
Unexpected dawn of joys untried;
Only to this wretched loving couple
Is the mutual happiness denied
Of our love without our understanding,
Seeing in our mate what is not there,
Always seeking happiness in daydream,
Faltering at an imagined scare.

Happy whom an empty dream engages,
Happy whose conjecture would be vain!
Every meeting, every glance, alas, enforces
Our dream, our conjecture yet again.
Tell me, what is Fate preparing for us?
Tell me, what so closely bound our life?
Oh, you were in ages long departed
Surely once my sister or my wife.

You knew every fibre of my being,
Studied how my purest nerve vibrates,
You could read me at a glance, whom mortal
Eye with so much labour penetrates;
On this hot blood you dripped moderation,
This wild wayward orbit you redressed
And in your angelic arms the comfort
Brought revival to this shattered breast;
You kept this man bound with magic lightness
And for him beguiled many a day.
O what blessedness was like those hours of rapture
When at your feet thankfully he lay,
Felt his heart against your own heart swelling,
Felt that your eyes looked and found him good,
Felt a brightening of all his senses
And a soothing of his stormy blood!

And of all that but a memory hovers
Yet awhile round the uncertain heart,
Feels the ancient truth within the same as ever,
And the new condition makes it smart.
And we seem to us but partly living,
Twilit round us is the brightest day.
Happy we, that Fate as it torments us
Yet can change us in no way!

A SONG OF MIGNON

  Only one who has yearned
   Can know my plight!
  Alone and quite cut off
   From all delight,
  I gaze upon the heavens
   Beyond the day.
  Ah! he who loves and knows me
   Is far away.
  My head swims and my vitals
   Burn me quite.
  Only one who has yearned
   Can know my plight!

from the novel Wilhelm Meister's Apprenticeship

AMOR AS LANDSCAPE PAINTER

On a lofty crag I sat at daybreak
And into the mist wide-eyed was staring;
Like an outstretched canvas primed with grey, it
Covered everything around, above me.

Then a lad sat himself down beside me,
Saying: My dear friend, how can you stare so
Wide-eyed, blankly at the empty canvas?
Have you really lost for ever all your
Joy in painting and in making pictures?

I looked at the child and thought in secret:
So the boy would see himself as master!

If you would remain thus dull and idle,
Said the lad, nothing will come of nothing;
Look, I'll paint you now a little picture,
Teach you how to paint a pretty picture.

And he pointed with his index finger
That by any other name was rosy,
Towards the fabric stretched out wide before him,
Started with his finger on a drawing.

At the top a lovely sun he painted,
By whose strong beams I was nearly dazzled,
And the gaps between the clouds he gilded,
Through the clouds he let the sunbeams filter;
Painted then the softly waving summits
Of the freshly quickened trees, drew hillsides
One after another, sketched beyond them;
Underneath he left no lack of water,
Drew the river so much after nature
That it seemed to glitter in the sunlight,
That it seemed to rush upon the sandbank.

Ah, there flowers were growing by the river,
And there colours glowed upon the meadow,
Gold, enamel, purple, something greenish,
Everything like emerald and garnet!
Bright and pure above he glazed the heavens
And the mountains, blue afar and further,
Till I, born anew and quite enchanted,
Gazed on now the painter, now the picture.

Well, he said, that was a demonstration
Of how fully this craft I have mastered;
But the hardest part is still to follow.

Thereupon he drew with pointed finger
And with great care, there upon the coppice,
At its far edge where the sun in splendour
Cast up from the bright ground its reflection,
Drew the maid, of all the most beloved,
Handsome and adorned with dainty garments,
Fresh her cheeks with her brown hair about them,
And her cheeks partook of that same colour
As the finger which had just portrayed them.

O you lad! I cried, what kind of master
Took you in his school to be his pupil,
That so quickly and so true to nature
Skilfully you start and well you finish?

Even as I speak, look, there a breeze is
Stirring and it sets the treetops swaying,
Ruffles all the waves upon the river,
Swells the veil of that quite perfect maiden
And – what startled me, already startled –
That maid now begins to move, her footsteps
Wend their way towards the very spot where
I am sitting with my wanton teacher.

Now that everything was set in motion –
Trees and river, flowers and now the veil, the
Dainty foot of all creation's fairest –
Do you really think that on my crag there
Crag-like I remained, unmoving, silent?

THE FIFTH
ROMAN ELEGY

Joyful on classical ground I am feeling new inspiration;
    Present and past I can hear louder, with greater allure.
Here I follow advice, I leaf through the works of the ancients
    With an industrious hand, daily enjoy them anew.
Night after night meanwhile I am otherwise busy with Amor;
    Though taught only by half, yet I get double delight.
Am I not self-taught as I study the form of a lovely
    Bosom and run my hand downward and over the hips?
Only then do I know about marble; I think, make connections,
    See with an eye that can feel, feel with a hand that can see.
Though my darling may rob me of one or two hours in the daytime,
    Hours in the night she gives in compensation to me.
We are not always kissing, sensible talk there is also;
    When she is taken by sleep, then I can lie and reflect.
Many a time have I lain in her arms and worked on a poem,
    Counting hexameters out tenderly over her back
With my fingers. And she in beautiful slumber is breathing
    And her breath is aglow right to the depths of my heart.
Amor is trimming the lamp and thinking of times when he rendered
    This very service for his trio of bards long ago.

NEARNESS OF HER BELOVED

I think of you when I see sunlight glitter
   Upon the ocean;
I think of you when shimmering brooklets set the
   Moonlight in motion.

I see you when above the distant roadway
   A dust cloud breaks;
At dead of night when on the narrow ridgeway
   The wanderer quakes.

I hear you when out there with a dull roaring
   The billows swell;
In the quiet grove I often walk and listen
   When all is still.

I am with you, however far you may be,
   To me you are near!
The sun sinks, soon the stars will shine above me.
   Would you were here!

BLESSED LONGING

Only to the wise man tell it
For the mob will soon make game:
I will praise the living creature
That desires a death by flame.

In the afterglow of love when
Once begotten, you begot,
Seeing the silent candle, by a
Strange emotion you are caught.

Then no longer by the shadows
Of the dark are you held down
For a new desire now draws you
To a higher union

And by distance undiscouraged
You came flying and are doomed
Till at last by light you lust for –
Butterfly – you are consumed.

But while you have not possessed
   This: Die and become!
You are but a dreary guest
   In this earthly gloom.

from West-Eastern Divan

Luxuriant on branches,
Beloved, what a scene!
Look at the fruit in bunches
With prickly husks and green.

Clenched, silent, long since hanging,
They know not what they are;
A bough is waving, swinging,
And rocking them with care.

Still the brown kernels ripen,
Their richness has begun
To move into the open,
Come out into the sun.

With joy now they are falling
Where husks burst with a snap;
So do my songs, my darling,
Drop heaped into your lap.

from West-Eastern Divan

GINGKO BILOBA

This tree, by the East entrusted
To my garden plot to grow,
Bears a leaf of secret meaning
That will nourish those who know.

Is it but one living being
That has split itself in twain?
Is it two that chose each other
Till we know the twain as one?

Such a question I have rightly
Understood, and answer: you
Surely from my songs have noticed
That I am both one and two?

from West-Eastern Divan

Marianne von Willemer

ZULEIKA: What's the meaning of this motion?
Does the east wind bring glad news?
For its pinions' bracing movement
On my heart's deep hurt sheds dews.

With the dust it plays caressing,
Starts it up in little clouds,
Drives towards the sheltered vine leaves
Happy insects in their crowds.

The sun's glow it gently softens,
My hot cheeks with coolness fills,
Kisses even in flight the vineyards
Glistening on fields and hills,

And its tender whisper comes from
Him who lovingly would greet;
Still before these hills grow darker
I'll sit silent at his feet.

Now fly on and serve the happy,
And the troubled try to move:
There, where lofty walls are glowing,
I shall find the one I love.

Oh, the heart's true tidings, wind of
Love, a fresh desire to live,
Come to me from his mouth only,
Nothing but his breath can give.

from Goethe's West-Eastern Divan

On the high-vaulted arches of the terrace
At one time he was walking to and fro;
The inscription carved once by his own dear hand there
I could not find, there is no more to show!

Oh close now, weary eyelids! In the twilight
Of that time, beautiful and far away,
My friend's high songs are ringing all around me,
And yesterday becomes for me today.

Invisible barriers, close yourselves about me;
In this charmed circle wherein once I moved
Now readily dissolve, my thoughts and senses:
Here I was happy, loving and beloved.

Friedrich Hölderlin

APPLAUSE
OF MEN

Sacred surely my heart, full of a fairer life,
Thanks to love? Tell me why you all thought more of me
    In my pride and my frenzy,
        Volubility, emptiness!

Oh, the crowd goes for what sells in the market-place,
And the servant respects only the powerful;
    Things divine are perceived by
        Only those who are so themselves.

HOME

With joy the boatman comes over calm seas home
From far-off islands where he has harvested;
    I'd gladly too be turning homeward;
        But, save my grief, what have I for harvest?

You lovely shores, O you that have brought me up,
Will you now calm love's griefs? Oh will you give me back,
    You forests of my childhood! at my
        Homecoming, quiet again to me now?

SOCRATES AND ALCIBIADES

'Why are you all the time, holiest Socrates,
Looking up to this youth? Don't you know greater things?
    Why with love do your glances
    Rest upon him as upon a god?'

Who most deeply has thought loves what is most alive,
Noble youth understands who has surveyed the world
    And the wise man will often
    Bow at last to the beautiful.

THE PARTING

Go our separate ways? All for the best, we thought?
If so, why did the act shock us as if we'd killed?
    Oh, how little our insight:
    We are ruled by a god within.

What! Betray him who first formed everything for us,
All our meaning and life, guardian god who brought
    Soul and sense to our love? No,
    This, this one thing I cannot do.

But the mind of the world thinks of another need,
Other iron demands lays down, and other laws,
    And our soul wears away from
    Day to day with the commonplace.

Yes! I knew in advance. Right from the time the deep
Rooted monster of fear came between gods and men,
    To appease it with blood the
    Hearts of lovers have had to die.

Let me speak not a word! Let me be blind to this
Deadly thing evermore! So may I move in peace
    Into solitude, so may
      We call parting our own at least.

Dearest, pass me the cup, that I may drink with you
Holy poison that saves, drink with you Lethe's drink,
    And enough to ensure that
      Hate and love are forgotten, all!

I will go now. Perhaps long after this we'll meet,
Diotima, once more. Then, though, desire will have
    Bled away and in peace like
      Blessed souls we shall walk about,

Strangers, this way and that where conversation leads,
Pensive, wavering, yet now the forgotten call
    Back this place of our parting,
      And within us a heart is warmed,

In amazement I look your way as voices, sweet
Singing ring in my ears, music of strings of old,
    And the lily is wafting
      Fragrance, golden above the stream.

Clemens Brentano

SPINNER'S SONG

Many a time and tide
Also the nightingale
Would sing its madrigal
When we were side by side.

I sing and cannot cry
And spin so lonely here
A thread that's pure and clear
While yet the moon shines high.

When we were side by side
We heard the nightingale,
You've gone, its madrigal
Reminds me, far and wide.

Whenever the moon's high
I think but of you here,
My heart is pure and clear,
God join us by and by!

Since you went far and wide
There's still the nightingale,
Telling in madrigal
How we were side by side.

God join us by and by,
So lonely I spin here,
The moon shines pure and clear,
I sing and long to cry!

Des Knaben Wunderhorn

My father told me
To rock the baby,
Tonight he'll cook me
Three eggs — well, maybe:
If he cooks me three
He'll eat two for me
And for just one egg
No rocking there'll be.

My mother told me
To spy on the maids,
Tonight she'll fry me
Three birds — well, try me!
If she fries me three
She'll eat two for me
And for just one bird
There's no treachery.

My sweetheart told me
To think about him,
Tonight he'll give me
Three kisses: doubt him?
If he gives me three,
More there'll surely be;
As for birds and eggs,
They won't bother me.

Adelbert von Chamisso

He, most glorious of mortals,
Oh how gentle, oh how kind,
Sweet of lips and clear of vision,
Firm of courage, bright of mind!

As in the blue depth above me
Bright and glorious is that star,
So he shines out in my heavens,
Bright and glorious, high and far.

Travel, travel on your pathways;
Just to gaze upon your light,
Just to gaze upon it humbly
Is my grief and my delight!

Do not hear my prayer, in silence
Offered for your happiness,
And ignore this lowly handmaid,
Glorious star of highest bliss!

Just the worthiest of all mortals
Should be honoured by your choice,
And she shall receive my blessing
Thousandfold as I rejoice.

I will be all tears and laughter,
Blessed, blessed shall I be;
Even though I suffer heartbreak –
Break, heart! What is that to me?

from Woman's Love and Life

Joseph von Eichendorff

FORMERLY

The tulips are in flower between the avenues
Where the white statues stand in silence among yews,
The fountain bounces balls of pure gold in its basin,
A sphinx lurks in the bower, amusingly to chasten.

Taking a turn today is Chloe – what a stunner! –
And there a gentleman politely waits upon her,
And just behind them both steals Cupid, keeping low,
Now ducking in the green, now aiming with his bow.

With gallant compliments he leans, the gentleman,
Sometimes she makes to strike the wanton with her fan;
Her taffeta rustles then, and then his buckles twinkle;
Often we hear a peal of pretty laughter tinkle.

But now from the château, across the pink sunset,
The musical clock strikes up a languid minuet,
So silent is the bower, he casts his kerchief down
And falls upon his knee with tender, earnest frown.

'What shall I do, oh, oh, how quickly it is darkling . . .'
'All the more easily can I see two stars sparkling . . .'
'What a bold gentleman!' 'Ah, Chloe, may I hope . . .?'
Then Cupid shoots his dart and with them all is up.

IMPATIENCE

In every tree's bark I would gladly carve it,
On every pebble gladly I'd engrave it,
In every fresh-turned plot I'd like to sow it
With cress-seed so that all would quickly know it,
On every scrap of paper write it plain:
My heart is yours, and ever shall remain.

And I would like to school a little starling
Till sharp and clear he spoke about my darling,
Until word-perfect he could speak my part
With all the ardent yearning of my heart;
Then he would warble through her window-pane:
My heart is yours, and ever shall remain.

I would instil it in the morning breeze
And whisper it among the stirring trees;
Oh, might it shine from every flower-star,
The scent bear it to her from near and far!
Waves, is it only mill-wheels you can entrain?
My heart is hers, and ever shall remain.

I thought it must be standing in my eyes,
My burning cheeks must all men recognize
And read what my dumb mouth may not declare,
And every breath would shout aloud to her
Who pays no heed to all this urgent pain:
My heart is yours, and ever shall remain!

GHAZAL

I am as flesh to spirit, as spirit to flesh for you,
I am as woman to man, as man to woman for you:
Whom else do you dare love when with eternal kisses
Far away from your lips I banish death for you?
I am your scent of roses, your song of nightingales,
I am your shaft of sunlight, the moon's disc for you:
What more do you want, what more do eyes of yearning seek?
Cast all, but all aside: you know I wait for you!

Annette von Droste-Hülshoff

YOUNG LOVE

Above the spring a bough is bobbing,
  Birds whistle overhead,
Wild anemone, pale blackthorn
  In the evening sun glow red,
And a young girl with golden ringlets
  Leans over the glittering wall,
Slender, of barely fifteen summers
  With the eyes of a timid gazelle.

Marigold petals she is plucking:
  'He loves me . . . he loves me not',
And when the oracle tells her ' . . . loves me'
  Her face is flushed and hot;
But 'loves me not' – oh, rage and horror!
  May heaven spare each bloom!
Grass and flowers and all the nosegay
  She flings to a watery doom.

Then to the plants her gaze turns sweetly
  Reflecting on things above:
The headstrong child of pious parents
  Who thinks of nothing but love,
This shy hind never knew another
  Bond than the bond of kin,
And now a boy who was not related –
  Is that not a grievous sin?

She sighs and sinks, bereft of courage
  In utter grief and shame,
And finally allows her stubborn
  Heart to be searched for blame.
A fantasy she now imagines:
  What if her house were on fire
And calls for help came from her mother
  And from her heart's desire?

Suddenly in a glistening downpour
  Pearls from her eyes rain forth,
Her gaze fixed on the plants as though to
  Suck the blood of the earth,
She wrings her little hands, and sobbing
  'Yes, yes, yes!' she exclaims;
'I'd save mamma, then to my lover
  I'd leap into the flames!'

SIX POEMS FROM *THE BOOK OF SONGS*

From my great woes I make
My little songs; they depart
Upon their sounding wings
And flutter to her heart.

They found their way to my love
Yet they come back and wail,
And wail, and what they saw
In her heart will not tell.

A fellow loves a girl who
Has chosen someone else;
This other loves another
And there are wedding bells.

The first man passing likely
The girl takes and for spite
Marries him; then the fellow
Is in a sorry plight.

The story is an old one
Yet it stays forever new;
And while it happens to someone
It breaks his heart in two.

They sat drinking tea round the table
And talked of love without cease.
The gentlemen spoke of aesthetics,
The ladies of tenderness.

Love, it must be platonic,
Said the councillor, high and dry.
The councillor's wife is ironic,
But for all that she breathes a sigh.

The canon opens his mouth wide:
Let love be not too rough,
Or else it is bad for the system.
The young lady murmurs: Enough!

The countess says in sorrow:
But love, love is a passion!
And to the baron she offers
A cup in benevolent fashion.

There was one more place at the table;
My darling, you were not there.
You would have told them so sweetly
About the love we share.

I do not know the meaning
Of why I am so sad;
I cannot get a legend
Of old times out of my head.

The air is cool, it is twilight,
And calmly flows the Rhine;
The top of the mountain sparkles
Where evening sunbeams shine.

The fairest maid is sitting
So wonderful up there,
Her golden jewels are flashing,
She is combing her golden hair.

With a golden comb she is combing
And singing the while a song;
There is a tune about it
That is both strange and strong.

In his small boat it seizes
The boatman with wild woe;
He is looking towards the heavens,
Not at the reefs below.

I believe the waves then swallow
Boatman and craft in one;
And that with her fine singing
The Lorelei has done.

Silent the night, the streets are sleeping,
This house was once my sweetheart's abode;
Long since from the town has she departed
But the house stands where it always stood.

A man stands there too, staring upward,
Wringing his hands in the grip of pain;
I shudder when I see his features –
The moon shows me my own face plain.

You double of mine, you pale companion!
Why do you ape my lover's woe
That tortured me where you are standing
So many nights so long ago?

※

    You are like a flower,
    So pure and fair and kind;
    I gaze at you, and sorrow
    Steals into my mind.

    I feel I should be laying
    Hands on your head and praying
    God that you may endure
    So kind and fair and pure.

Eduard Mörike

A GIRL'S FIRST LOVE SONG

Look! What is in the creel?
But my hands shake:
Do I grasp a sweet eel?
Do I grasp a snake?

Love is a blind
Fisherwoman;
Says to the youngster,
Where is it coming?

To my hands it rushes!
Grief! Joy! I am possessed!
It twists and turns, fastens
Upon my breast.

O wonder! It boldly
Bites through my skin:
O love, I am frightened —
It is slipping within!

What to do, where to start? For
The terrible thing
Is thrashing about as
It curls in a ring.

I must have poison —
It girds its domain,
Sinks blissfully deeper
And oh, I am slain!

THE FORSAKEN MAID

When the cocks crow, before
   The stars expire,
I must be at the range,
   Must light the fire.

Lovely the gleam of the flames,
   And the sparks leap;
But I stare into them,
   My sorrow deep.

Suddenly it comes to me,
   You faithless lad:
I dreamed of you last night —
   Such dreams I had.

And now tears upon tears
   Down my cheeks rain:
Day comes — oh might it go
   Away again!

FAIR ROHTRAUT

What is King Ringang's daughter called?
   Rohtraut, Fair Rohtraut.
What does she do then all the day
When spinning and sewing are not her way?
   She fishes and hunts.
Oh that her hunter I might be!
Fishing and hunting were all to me.
   — Hush, quiet, my heart!

When but a little time was past,
   Rohtraut, Fair Rohtraut,
A lad in the castle met the need,
In hunting garb, upon a steed
   To hunt with Rohtraut.
Oh would I were the son of a king!
Rohtraut, Fair Rohtraut makes my heart sing.
   – Hush, quiet, my heart!

They tarried a while beneath an oak,
   And Fair Rohtraut laughed:
Why in such rapture do you stare?
Very well, kiss me if you dare!
   Oh! the lad took fright.
And yet he thinks: I'm permitted this,
And on Rohtraut's mouth he sets a kiss.
   – Hush, quiet, my heart!

In silence then they cantered home,
   Rohtraut, Fair Rohtraut.
Never so joyful had the lad been:
Even today were you made queen
   I would not be vexed;
You leaves of the forest know the truth,
I've kissed Fair Rohtraut on the mouth.
   – Hush, quiet, my heart!

DOMESTIC
SCENE

A bedroom. Schoolmaster Ciborius and his young wife. The light is out.

'Rike, are you asleep?' 'Not yet.' 'Have you bottled the gherkins?'
'Yes.' 'How much did you take out of my vinegar store?'
'Less than two measures full.' 'What! Two measures nearly? And from
  Which jar – not from the one left of the sill in the yard?'
'Certainly.' 'Damn! I must do my experiment from the beginning
  Just as I'd hoped I would see something by way of result!
How about asking me first?' 'You were teaching.' 'You could have waited.'
  'Darling, the cucumbers were over-ripe as it was.'
'Not long ago I said: for household use, number seven . . .'
  'Oh, who ever could keep numbers like that in his head!'
'Seven is easy to keep; there is nothing simpler than seven!
  One big arabic sign, clear on the label it shows.'
'But you keep changing its place as the sun goes from window to window;
  When I am pressed at the stove there is no time for a search.
Dearest, your vinegar brew will one day bring me to madness!
  Putting up with so much, I have been patient till now.
When you installed yourself in the laundry where space is restricted,
  With your still and your fire, that was the limit, I thought.
I was not happy to see on the bench your retorts and your jars there
  Pushing my mignonettes, roses and stock to the side;
Now instead round the house there are standing at every window
  Bellies of glass in ranks, swathed to the middle in straw:
Four of them plumb in my way on the hearth, and half up the chimney
  Hangs such a monster now – one more experiment yet!
We'll be a laughing-stock . . . I'm sorry, but . . .' 'What are you saying?
  Laughing-stock?' 'You missed what the dean's wife said today,
And in each of her words I could hear the tones of the mocker:
  Wicked he is, and the head's brother-in-law, what is more.'
'Well?' 'Like a fortress she said that the schoolmaster's house was, a bulwark

She called my balcony here, said it was bristling with guns!'
'Mean talk that, out of purest envy! I hope to maintain my
    Hobby as long as I'm here, just like her consort the dean.
He has a passion for birds – for canaries and others in cages –
    Dozens: my passion remains vinegar properly made.'

Pause. He seems thoughtful. She speaks aside:

'Truly I'm sorry for him: he is troubled by the assistant
    Master who poses a threat, someone he never could trust.'

He continues:

'I have always performed my duty as schoolmaster: look no
    Further than recent grades made by my pupils in class.
What on the physical plane I think some day of achieving
    For the professions, the state, during the hours I am free –
Though for my family I guarantee no important advantage,
    For the time being at least – that I am silent about;
But . . . let me meet that man who denies a downtrodden teacher
    Harmless delights such as this, making a vinegar brew!
Who speaks of trivial things, of absurdities – be he the rector
    Or the headmaster, or yet the district inspector of schools –
Let him grapple with me, I will deal with him! Oh, you will find me
    Armed to the teeth, my breast girded with three coats of mail!
– Rike, you're laughing! You can't conceal it: the mattress is shaking!
    What is the matter? Are you mocking me now, silly girl?'
'Darling, silly, most precious of men! I can't keep a straight face:
    I would never have sought passion in vinegar so!'
'That is enough of your jokes! For me it's a serious matter.'
    'Steady, old fellow, and let's settle our argument now.
There is no pleasure for me in removing what most you delight in:
    It's too important to you, that much I quite understand.
If you look from your desk in the schoolhouse out of the window
    Over the yard at those treasures of yours, the retorts,

All with the midday sun in its glory shining upon them,
   Warming to ripeness your wine secretly as it ferments:
Well, your heart and your eye are quickened – though not very often –
   Which my most colourful stock never has managed to do;
And a pipe of tobacco before this agreeable vision
   Takes you away from your cares better than anything else;
Yes, since you've been preparing with your own vinegar that red
   Ink which would otherwise cost quite a few pennies or more,
I believe that the chaos of exercise books has become less
   Hateful to you; you are soothed by their familiar smell.
How could I cheat you of this? You just overdo it a little.
   All things – your proverb declares – have their own measure and goal.'
'Leave me! When one day my product makes you a prosperous woman . . .'
   'Dearest, that's what you said when we had silkworms in here.'
'Am I to blame that the fodder gave out, that the animals perished?'
   'Any new enterprise brings with it risks of its own.'
'Don't you allow for the name, and for the fame of the author?'
   'Fame in plenty we had; then came our vinegar brew.'
'I am a Corresponding Member of three associations.'
   'If but one of them took some of your jars every year!'
'You are not capable of any rational argument, are you!'
   'Well, since you are, you will need salad whenever you sup.'
'Thankless! All I produce is splendid in every variety.'
   'Numbers seven and nine . . . these I would not recommend.'
'I have noticed today that you like to trump me in verses.'
   'Were they not verses, then, you have been speaking till now?'
'That is an occupational weakness, and you will abuse it?'
   'I cannot help, like you, talking in metre like this.'
'I have been practising hard to spice inoffensive exchanges.'
   'Yes, but in serious talk pretty peculiar it sounds.'
'That being so, I forbid it: speak to me straight from the shoulder.'
   'Right; let us see how prose mixes with Classical verse.'
'Nonsense! Now let us stop. Contending with women is fruitless.'

'Fruitless, that's what I call making your vinegar, dear.'
'Still your pentameter steps where its foot brings me its conclusion!'
'Your hexameter trots after it, cannot resist.'
'Oh, if it suits you to have still the last word, only the last one,
   Have it! I swear you have heard such a word spoken by me.'
'As for me, a hexameter can stand quite independent.'

Silence. The husband grows restless, he is clearly troubled not to have heard the end of the couplet or not to have completed it himself. A little later his wife laughs and comes to his aid:

'I've been too hard on you. Really, your vinegar's good;
If in future it turns out better still, then it's only
   You it is due to, with your surely unquarrelsome wife!'

He too laughs heartily and kisses her:

'Rike, first thing tomorrow I'll clear the front windows completely
   And in the fireplace your hams will be resplendent alone!'

Theodor Storm

HYACINTHS

Far away, music; here is silence, night,
I breathe a scent of slumber from the plants;
You are for ever in my spirit's sight
And I would like to sleep, but you must dance.

The music raves on without interval,
The candles burn on and the fiddles screech,
The dancers part, then for each other reach,
And all are glowing; only you are pale.

And you must dance; as strange arms are thrown out
To clasp your bosom: oh, let no one hurt you!
I see your white dress as it flies about
With your slight form, your vulnerable virtue . . .

More sweetly streaming comes the scent of night,
More dreamily from the chalice of the plants;
You are for ever in my spirit's sight,
And I would like to sleep, but you must dance.

In words you do not want to say it
But put your burning mouth on mine
And from your pulse so deeply throbbing
A lovely secret I divine.

You timid dove, you flee before me
But on my breast press yourself hard;
To love you are already victim
And yet you barely know the word.

From me you bend your slender body
While your red mouth bestows a kiss;
Yourself you are intent on saving
But that self is quite lost by this.

You feel there is no going back now
So why still do you shy away?
You must discharge the obligation,
You must, in full, you must, I say.

Yearning by half and by half anxious,
By now the cup is brimming high;
That modesty awaits possession
Until in love it is to die.

A LESSON

The sun is shining: put your courtship by!
For love is like the timidest of women
Who will not let her eyes be pools to swim in
But will remain a riddle or will die.
Yet when the evening silently slips down,
Ah, then the rule of tender thoughts draws near;
When into sweet confusion all is thrown
By spreading dusk, and forms become unclear,
Ah, then the hand, the mouth quite lightly stray
And what was bold by half has all its way.

Klaus Groth

WHERE THERE'S A WILL

No ditch is so wide and no wall is so high,
If two love each other, then they will get by.

No storm is so wild and no night is so dark,
If two want to meet, they will soon reach the mark.

There's bound to be moonlight, or maybe a star,
A torch or a lantern will light where they are.

There's always a ladder, a plank, come what may,
If two are in love they will find out a way.

Conrad Ferdinand Meyer

LETHE

Lately in a dream I saw a vessel
Oarless on the waters make its way.
Stream and sky glowed dimly like the breaking
Or like the departure of the day.

Lads and slender girls sat, these were leaning
Overboard, with lotus those were crowned,
And I saw that each of them was drinking
From a gleaming bowl that went around.

Now a song full of sweet sorrow sounded,
Which the band of wreathed companions sang —
And I recognized your neck bowed meekly,
And your voice that through the chorus rang.

In the waves I dived: chilled to the marrow,
Their strange coolness I could barely stand.
But I reached the gently moving vessel,
Thrust myself among the sacred band.

And I saw it was your turn for drinking,
And you lifted up the brimming bowl,
Said to me, familiarly winking:
'Here's to you forgetting me, dear soul!'

A defiant fit of love drove me to
Snatch the bowl and toss it in the flood:
Down it sank, and see! a touch of colour
Tinged your cheek as with a glow of blood.

You gave me your pallid mouth: I kissed it,
Wild with grief, could not be comforted.
Then in my embrace you melted smiling,
And I knew once more that you are dead.

Richard Dehmel

Two people are walking through a bare, cold grove;
the moon runs with them far above.
The moon exceeds the oak trees' height;
no cloud obscures the heavenly light
towards which rise black mountain peaks.
The voice of a woman speaks:

I'm carrying, and not from you,
in sin I'm walking at your side.
Against myself did I transgress.
I stopped believing in happiness,
yet by deep longing I was tried
for something in life, maternal bliss
and duty; so I took a chance
and made my sex all look askance —
went with a man I did not know
and got then in this blessed state.
But now comes the revenge of fate:
now I have met my darling, you.

She walks on with an awkward stride.
She looks up: the moon runs beside.
In light her dark look soon is drowned.
Then from a man's throat comes the sound:

The child you have conceived, it shall
not be a burden to your soul:
oh see, how bright the heaven shimmers!

There is a radiance in the weather;
on a cold sea we drift together,
yet of itself a warm stream glimmers
from you towards me, from me towards you.
It will transfigure the stranger's child
you will have borne to me, from me;
you have brought radiance back to me,
restored to me my childhood's light.

He clasps her round her sturdy hips.
In the cold air they join their lips.
Two people are walking through a high, bright night.

from Two People

Stefan George

If I do not touch you today
The thin thread of my soul will sever —
A bowstring that can bear no more.
Let signs of love be veils of sorrow
To one all yours with no tomorrow.
Tell: should such torment come my way?
Sprinkle some coolness on the fever
Of one who dithers at your door.

from The Book of The Hanging Gardens

You pure and slender as a flame
You as the morning soft and clear
You flowering scion of noble name
You as a spring arcane and sheer

Walking with me in sunny meads
Thrilling me under evening skies
Giving me light among the shades
O you cool wind O you hot sighs

You are my wish and all I think
I breathe you in with every breeze
I lap you up with every drink
I kiss you with all fragrances

You flowering scion of noble name
You as a spring arcane and sheer
You pure and slender as a flame
You as the morning soft and clear.

from The New Realm

BIM BAM BONG

A clang wings birdlike through the night,
   at flying he's no failure;
o'er hill and dale he takes his flight
   in Catholic regalia.

He's looking for the she-clang BIM
   whose flight has far outpaced him –
i.e., the matter is most grim:
   another has displaced him.

'Oh come,' he calls, 'your faithful BAM
   is pining since we parted:
oh come back, BIM, beloved lamb,
   your BAM is broken-hearted!'

But BIM, to let you know it all,
   has fallen for BONG's flatteries:
he is an Evangelical
   and that's just what the matter is.

Poor BAM flies onward through the night
   high over wood and clearing.
But, alas, all in vain his flight
   for he has faulty steering.

THE TWO PARALLELS

Two parallels were heading
straight for infinity,
two souls of law-abiding
respectability.

They sought no intersection
before their blessed grave:
until that last connection
they vowed they would behave.

But after they had wandered
ten light-years side by side
the lonely couple pondered
anew their earthly pride.

Were they still parallel? They
themselves were not sure, quite;
together like two souls they
flowed through eternal light.

That light, he overpowered them
and they were one in him;
eternity devoured them
just like two seraphim.

Hugo von Hofmannsthal

THE TWO OF THEM

She bore the goblet in her hand —
Her chin and mouth curved like its lip;
So light and steady was her gait
The goblet did not even drip.

So light and steadfast was his hand:
Upon a quick young horse he rode
And with a careless gesture he
Mastered it till it trembling stood.

But when he was about to take
The same light goblet from her hand
It was too heavy for them both:
The two of them began to quake,
Till hand by hand could not be found
And dark wine spilt upon the ground.

Rainer Maria Rilke

LOVE SONG

How shall I hold my soul so that
it does not touch on yours? And how shall I
lift it up over you to other things?
Ah, gladly would I settle it
with some lost object in the night
at a strange silent spot that sings
no answer when your depths are stirred and cry.
Yet all that touches on us, me and you,
takes us together as a bow
draws from two strings a single sound.
Upon what instrument have we been strung?
What player holds us in his hand?
Oh sweet the song.

LEDA

The god took its shape in his hour of need
then almost swooned to find the swan so fair;
in it he let his crazed self disappear.
But his deception drove him to the deed

before he'd tried the creature as a sure
vessel of feelings. And the opened one
now recognized her guest within the swan
and knew now: he was asking for

what she, crazed in her struggle to withstand,
could hide no more. He swooped, they were together
his neck thrust through her ever-failing hand

the god in the beloved let himself come.
Then for the first time he rejoiced in feather
and became truly swan deep in her womb.

Georg Heym

Your eyelashes, so long,
Your eyes' dark waters,
Let me dive into them,
Let me go deep down.

If the miner goes below
And his dim lamp sways
Over the gate of metals,
High on the wall of shadow,

See, I climb down
To forget in your arms,
Far from what drones above,
Brightness, torment, day.

In the fields
Where the wind stops, drunk on corn,
A high thorn twists, high and sick
Against the sky's blue.

Give me your hand,
We want to grow together,
Prey to one wind,
A flight of lonely birds,

Hearing in summer
The organ of dull storms,
Bathing in autumn light
On the shore of the blue day.

Sometimes we want to stand
At the edge of the dark well,
To gaze deep into the silence
In search of our love.

Or we will step out
From the shade of golden weeds,
Tall into a sunset
That gently touches your brow.

Divine grief,
Don't speak of eternal love,
Raise your tankard,
Drink sleep.

Once to stand at the end
Where ocean with yellowish flecks
Lightly rolls already
Into September's bay.

To rest above
In the house of thirsty flowers,
Down over the cliffs
The wind sings and trembles.

But from the poplar
Towering in the eternal blue
A brown leaf falls already,
Settles on your neck.

EVE BLOSSOM HAS WHEELS
Merz-poem 1

O thou, beloved of my twenty-seven senses,
I love thine!
Thou thee thee thine, I thine, thou mine, we?
That (by the way) is beside the point!
Who art thou, uncounted woman,
Thou art, art thou?
People say, thou werst,
Let them say, they don't know what they are talking about.
Thou wearest thine hat on thy feet, and wanderest on thine hands,
On thine hands thou wanderest.
Hallo, thy red dress, sawn into white folds,
Red I love eve Blossom, red I love thine!
Thou thee thee thine, I thine, thou mine, we?
That (by the way) belongs to the cold glow!
eve Blossom, red eve Blossom, what do people say?
Prize Question: 1. eve Blossom is red.
                  2. eve Blossom has wheels.
                  3. what colour are the wheels?
Blue is the colour of your yellow hair,
Red is the whirl of your green wheels,
Thou simple maiden in everyday dress,
Thou small green animal,
I love thine!
Thou thee thee thine, I thine, thou mine, we?
That (by the way) belongs to the glowing brazier!
eve Blossom,

eve,
E-V-E,
E easy, V victory, E easy,
I trickle your name.
Your name drops like soft tallow.
Do you know it, eve,
Do you already know it?
One can also read you from the back.
And you, you most glorious of all,
You are from the back as from the front,
E-V-E.
Easy victory.
Tallow trickles to strike over my back!
eve Blossom,
Thou drippy animal,
I
Love
Thine!
I love you!!!

Author's translation
edited by Stefan Themerson

Erich Kästner

ODE TO JOY
by her chamber virtuoso

You ninthmost of my symphonies!
When you have on that pink-striped shift which clings . . .
Come like a cello, fit between my knees
And let me stroke your sympathetic strings.

Let me leaf through your manuscript and score –
I'm hot to Handel, put me on your Liszt:
I'd like to trumpet you to every shore,
My triple-tongued delight, not to be missed!

Come, through the octaves let us take a stand!
(The furioso, please, just once again!)
May I accompany you with my left hand?
At the crescendo let me take the strain!

O diapason closing full! O swell!
I love to feel how your heart skips a beat!
A touch on your well-tempered clavicle . . .
And at the stretto may our motions meet!

Mascha Kaléko

PIHI

About the *pihi* I have lately heard,
In China reckoned a prodigious bird.
It has but one wing: always two by two
Go flocks of *pihi* in the distant blue.
The bird can take off only in a pair
And it is grounded in the singular.
– My soul is like the *pihi*, never free,
Chained to the nest if you abandon me.

Ernst Jandl

PAIN THROUGH
FRICTION

```
                    frau
                   frfrauau
                  frfrfrauauau
                 frfrfrfrauauauau
                frfrfrfrfrauauauauau
               frfrfrfrfrfrauauauauauau
              frfrfrfrfrfrfrauauauauauauau
             frfrfrfrfrfrfrfrauauauauauauauau
```

NOTES

A search through three recent international anthologies of love poetry produced one German lyric: this book seeks to make up for the oversight. Because it is more for lovers than scholars (though one hopes the latter will get something out of it), titles are sometimes silently editorial and notes have been kept to a minimum.

The love celebrated in this book is the erotic variety, Donne's 'fast balme' between two people of usually different sexes; the deliberate blurring of sacred and profane love characteristic of much Baroque poetry is also represented. It seemed best to arrange the poems in chronological order, to allow the reader to make connections against a historical background of eight centuries. The selection is inevitably personal, though I have tried too to reflect general taste by including poems that regularly appear in German anthologies. Reading German poetry one is never far from music: a few poems are here mainly through musical associations. The sign ♪ refers to some musical settings of the original texts.

The translations (which are not for singing) are as close as is readable. On the whole, I have rhymed where the original does, though Goethe's bear in 'Lili's Park' must growl unrhymed, and I have mostly abandoned feminine rhymes where they alternate à la française with masculine rhymes, because English simply does not have enough feminine rhymes for serious occasions, and reproducing all rhymes with usually masculine English counterparts would have interrupted the rhythmic flow. As for metre in general, I have most often matched it because of linguistic kinship, though a concern for equivalence before equality has occasionally led me to do otherwise. With poems in adapted Classical metres I have attempted something similar in English: such metres, disregarded by most English poets, produced some of the greatest early nineteenth-century German poetry.

One of these translations was first published in my booklet *Dark Summer* (Menard Press, 1976), one was broadcast in my BBC World Service series 'The Poetry of Europe' (1981), one was done for a Dutch-Finnish translators' conference (1981), and some appeared at various times on concert programmes and record sleeves. The translation 'Luxuriant on branches' won first prize in an English Goethe Society competition (1982). Leonard Forster's and Arthur Hatto's readings of medieval German texts were indispensable, as were James Boyd's and David Luke's studies of Goethe. Many poems were brought to my notice by my publisher and his friends; my old teacher Michael Hamburger cleared up a textual problem in Hölderlin; Peter F. Smith advised on George and Rilke; Shui Chien-tung applied considerable learning to Kaléko's *pihi*. To other friends and colleagues and not least my wife Satu, my thanks; all remaining blemishes are my responsibility.

p. 11 'You're for me': from a collection of model letters, this famous poem suggests how a woman might write to the man she loves.

p. 11 *Floret silva undique*: the third line translates the first. This and the preceding poem (*Wær diu werlt alliu mîn*) from the collection *Carmina Burana* ♪ Orff, 1937.

p. 12 'Siegfried meets Kriemhild': a tender moment near the beginning of the epic of murder and revenge which inspired Wagner's *Ring*. The metre shares roots with Anglo-Scottish ballad metre.

p. 14 The Austrian Der von ('He of') Kürenberc wrote *Minnelieder* ('songs of courtly love') just before Troubadour techniques arrived from southern France, as we can tell from the old Germanic form of his poem translated here. A jess (*riemen*) is a strap tied round a falcon's feet to hold it on the fist; cf. the sculptor's name Riemenschneider ('jess-cutter').

p. 15 Henric van Veldeke was a contemporary of the foregoing from further west. He was a native of Limburg, the province now divided between Belgium and the Netherlands; there is a square named after him in Maastricht. His dialect is an ancestor of Dutch. His work shows the influence of the Troubadours: his forms are elegant, as is his joke against Tristan.

p. 17 'The Lover'. The three stanzas show three aspects of the beloved: as a carefree country girl; as a young woman finding that her lover is still alive; as a (probably married) lady teasing her lover. The elaborate form – displayed here more clearly than in most German editions – resembles those of Heinrich's contemporary, the *maestre dels trobadors* Giraut de Borneil.

pp. 19–21 Two dawn songs from the heyday of the *Minnesang*; Wolfram von Eschenbach is better known for the romance *Parzival* which inspired Wagner. A dawn song was originally an *alba* or aubade sung by a *joglar* ('player, performer', whence later 'juggler') in his role of watchman, to warn his master the *trobador* ('finder', inventor of songs) that any time now his lady's husband could be back from a crusade, or his henchmen could check on her, or tongues could start wagging; courtly love was an odd amalgam of St Bernard of Clairvaux's cult of Mary, and adultery. Heinrich's poem is a dialogue between the lover and his lady after the watchman's warning. Wolfram, standing further back, gives a dialogue between watchman and lady (presumably the lover is still asleep) until the last stanza, when the poet himself describes a touching farewell.

p. 22 Walther von der Vogelweide, an Austrian, was the most versatile lyric poet of his time. 'Under the Lime Tree' (*Under der linden* ♪ F. Martin, 1960) is spoken by a peasant girl flattered on being called Noble Lady.

p. 24 Gottfried von Strassburg wrote the fullest account in verse of the Tristan legend, which from obscure Celtic origins had been adapted during the twelfth century as a romance for the entertainment of lords and ladies by northern French poets, whose metre Gottfried echoes.

p. 24 'The Noble Heart' is from Gottfried's Prologue. 'Half a century before the Bolognese Guido Guinizelli conceived his humane and thus anti-feudal philosophy of the *cuore gentile*, the Strassburger Gottfried formulated his doctrine of the *edelez herze*, which similarly opened the doors to those of the highest culture, whatever their social origins' (Arthur Hatto).

p. 25 'Lamer': Tristan and Isolde are sailing from Ireland to Cornwall, unaware that they have quenched their thirst with a love potion intended for her and the elderly King Mark, whom she is to marry.

p. 25 '*l'amer* was love': *amer* is here an early form of *aimer*.

p. 27 The Ballad of the Royal Children is one of the most widespread products of central European oral tradition; it travelled to Scandinavia and even to Finland, where over a hundred versions have been recorded. Its source and date are unknown. Its resemblance to the story of Hero and Leander has led some scholars to suggest a Renaissance origin. The version translated here was printed in the nineteenth century, when folklore was in vogue.

p. 29 Weckherlin is the earliest German poet of note who can be described as Baroque. Like the Minnesingers four hundred years before, he turned to France for models. After generations of Protestant hymn-writing, he wrote about sexual love (among other things) and explored the French alexandrine, as in his sonnet translated here – though it works better in English with twelve syllables reduced to ten. This is one of the earliest German sonnets, at least in structure; its use of repeated words instead of rhymes recalls the sestina. Weckherlin settled in England, where he served under Cromwell as Latin (i.e. Foreign) Secretary; his successor was Milton.

p. 30 Opitz established international ideas and canons of taste in German language and literature. He learnt much from Weckherlin, who in turn learnt from him. 'To his Coy Mistress' anticipates Marvell's poem.

p. 31 'The Platonick Lover' (the original is untitled) blurs, in typically Baroque manner, conventional distinctions between sacred and profane love. 'Alcmene's son' is Hercules. 'My light' (*Mein Licht*) recalls the *mea lux* of the Roman love poet Propertius (Elegies, 2:28); cf. Ezra Pound, 'Homage to Sextus Propertius', IX.

p. 32 Fleming was a diplomat whose travels to Estonia and Persia freed him from poetic conventions at home.

p. 33 Gryphius was the leading lyric and dramatic poet of his time. Behind his sonnet in alexandrines translated here one may glimpse the conflagrations of the Thirty Years War.

p. 34 'On the Mouth'. The word 'alicant' (*Alikant*) appeared in English in 1500: meaning originally a Spanish wine from Alicante, its Arabic form made it (as here) a synonym of 'elixir'. Hofmannswaldau was born and died in Breslau.

p. 34 'Jewish': texts vary between *der Juden* ('of the Jews') and *der Inden* ('of the Indies'); the two names look virtually identical in Gothic type.

p. 35 Von Zesen was the son of a vicar and studied at the University of Wittemberg. 'On the Eyes of his Love' is a sonnet in the manner of – and comparable with – Camões' *De quantas graças tinha, a Natureza* or Góngora's *Mientras por competir con tu caballo*.

p. 36 Stolle was born in Silesia and became Professor of Law in Jena. 'Love's Metamorphosis': the salamander, a kind of lizard, was thought to be so cold-blooded that it could survive fire and even put it out. It was a favourite metaphor of Baroque poets throughout Europe.

p. 37 Günther was highly valued by Goethe, despite his allegedly dissolute life. Later scholarship inclines to the view that one who wrote so much in his short life could not have been that dissolute.

p. 40 'Gather ye Rosebuds' rehearses the Horatian theme of *carpe diem* in rhythms reminiscent of Herrick. Gleim was an *Anakreontiker*, celebrating the good life usually in the trochaic metre of his ancient Greek model.

p. 41 Goethe pursued 'the Eternal Feminine' (*das Ewig-Weibliche*) throughout his long career. Of the thirteen poems translated here, the first was written when he was eighteen, the last when he was sixty-six.

p. 42 'Welcome and Parting': *Willkommen und Abschied* ♪ Schubert, D767.

p. 43 'The Violet': *Das Veilchen* ♪ Mozart, K476.

p. 44 'Gretchen at the spinning-wheel, alone': the stage direction in *Faust*. *Gretchen am Spinnrade* ♪ Schubert, D118.

p. 45 'Lili's Park' recalls Book 10 of the *Odyssey*, in which Circe, surrounded by wild beasts she has drugged, turns the hero's men into pigs. Here the young poet visits a formal garden which is also a private zoo belonging to a Frankfurt merchant's teenage daughter he is in love with. Among her elegant friends he feels closer to her animals, seeing himself as a performing bear that gives its paw (*menotte*) in greeting, knows it is an object of ridicule but is hopelessly devoted to its mistress. In consolation – or is it? – Lili smears her pet's lips with 'jungle juice' (a guess at the mysterious *Balsam-Feuer*). The poem is memorable as a light-hearted portrayal of humiliation in love.

p. 50 'To Charlotte von Stein', written in the spring following the autumn of 'Lili's Park', shows the poet celebrating his love for an older woman. The platonic liaison was to last ten years, until Goethe's departure for Italy.

p. 52 'A Song of Mignon': the wraith-like figure's lyric *Nur wer die Sehnsucht kennt* ♪ Beethoven, WoO134; Schubert, D310, 359, 481, 877; Schumann, Op. 98a; Tchaikovsky, Op. 6; Wolf, 1888.

p. 52 'Amor as Landscape Painter': one of the first fruits of Goethe's Italian tour (1786–8). This account of an imaginary picture's evolution uses the narrative approach of the early Renaissance (e.g. Dante) to a serious subject; but Goethe has neither rhyme nor stanza.

p. 55 'The Fifth Roman Elegy': one of twenty marking the start of Goethe's 'Classical' period. The form is the elegiac couplet of the three Roman love poets Catullus, Tibullus and Propertius, the 'trio' of this elegy's last line.

p. 55 'Here I follow advice': Horace's in the *Ars Poetica* – 'As for you, peruse Greek models by night, by day' (*Vos exemplaria Graeca / nocturna versate manu, versate diurna*) – though Goethe goes on to say he follows only half of the Roman's advice.

p. 56 'Nearness of her Beloved': literally 'the Beloved', but the article is masculine, for the poet is speaking as a woman. *Nähe des Geliebten ♪* Schubert, D162.

p. 56 'Blessed Longing' recalls a Persian motif (now universal) of the moth and the flame, though Goethe speaks of a butterfly.

p. 57 The *West-Eastern Divan* (1814–15) is the lyric climax of Goethe's later years, a volume (the original meaning of the Persian word) somewhat in the manner of the fourteenth-century Persian poet Hâfiz, while the forms show a return to native German metres after Goethe's Classical period.

p. 57 'Luxuriant on branches': the person addressed is Marianne von Willemer (see below).

p. 58 'Ginkgo biloba' uses the fan-shaped, grooved leaf of the maidenhair tree as a metaphor of love. Of Chinese origin, this plant – of which there is only one species – is used medicinally to stimulate circulation.

p. 59 Marianne von Willemer, young wife of a Frankfurt banker, is the beloved Zuleika (a conventional name in Persian poetry) of Goethe's *West-Eastern Divan*. She collaborated in several poems, and some are her own work, adopted by Goethe after his (not always happy) emendations. This poem is translated from her original text.

p. 60 'Memorial': engraved on a tablet in the gardens of Heidelberg Castle, where Marianne and Goethe spent a few days in September 1815. The original runs:

> Auf der Terrasse hochgewölbten Bogen
> War eine Zeit sein Kommen und sein Gehn;
> Die Chiffre, von der lieben Hand gezogen,
> Ich fand sie nicht, sie ist nicht mehr zu sehn!
>
> O schließt euch nun, ihr müden Augenlider!
> Im Dämmerlicht der fernen, schönen Zeit

> Umtönen mich des Freundes hohe Lieder;
> Zur Gegenwart wird mir Vergangenheit.
> Schließt euch um mich, ihr unsichtbaren Schranken;
> Im Zauberkreis, der magisch mich umgibt,
> Versenkt euch willig, Sinne und Gedanken;
> Hier war ich glücklich, liebend und geliebt.

p. 61 Hölderlin, in his tragically brief career, idealized ancient Greece even more than did his predecessors and was more venturesome in his use of Classical metres. Of the poems translated here, 'Home' is in alcaics, the rest are in asclepiads. The first three – *Menschenbeifall, Die Heimat, Sokrates und Alcibiades* – ♪ Britten, Op. 61.

p. 62 'Socrates and Alcibiades': the philosopher is rebuked for his infatuation with his beautiful, talented, rich pupil, and he defends himself. In the second stanza, Britten has set the now discredited *Tugend* ('virtue') instead of *Jugend* ('youth').

p. 64 'Spinner's Song': the repetitions enact the monotony of the girl's work. Brentano reported being moved to tears by the memory of his mother singing as she spun: 'Once when I heard her singing, a nightingale at our window also began to sing; it was already very late, and the moon was shining clear and bright. But my mother did not stop singing, and the bird and she sang together.'

p. 65 *Des Knaben Wunderhorn* ('The Lad's Wondrous Horn') is a collection of lyrics based on German folk poetry edited by Clemens Brentano and his brother-in-law Achim von Arnim. Many such collections appeared throughout Europe during the second half of the eighteenth and the first half of the nineteenth centuries, and countless poets – especially in Germany and England – wrote lyrics and ballads in 'folk' style: examples are Goethe's *Erlkönig* and Coleridge's 'Rime of the Ancient Mariner'. *Des Knaben Wunderhorn* is the source of Brahms' 'Lullaby' (Op. 49) and of over twenty Mahler settings.

p. 65 'My father told me': *Hat gesagt – bleib's nicht dabei* ♪ Reger, Op. 75; R. Strauss, Op. 36.

p. 66 'Woman's Love and Life' strikes us today as a disingenuous work, a sequence of poems about the crucial stages of a woman's life, spoken by her but written by a man. *Frauenliebe und -leben* ♪ Schumann, Op. 42; of his cycle of eight lyrics, the second (*Er, der Herrlichste von allen*) is translated here, and mischievously quoted by Schwitters (q.v.).

p. 67 'Formerly': a mock-Rococo fantasy in alexandrines. *Sonst* ♪ Pfitzner, Op. 15.

p. 68 'Impatience': *Ungeduld* ♪ Schubert, D795.

p. 69 The Graf von Platen published three collections of *ghazals*. The even-numbered lines of the *ghazal* (a form of Arab origin) rhyme with the opening couplet; the translation here can only echo the rhymes (*Leibe dir / Weibe dir*, etc.). The form is much used by Hâfiz, as is the conventional image of rose and nightingale.

p. 70   Annette von Droste-Hülshoff is considered the leading German woman poet of the nineteenth century. Contrast 'Young Love' with the poem by Walther von der Vogelweide on p. 23.

p. 72   Heine's early lyrics, collected into 'The Book of Songs' (*Das Buch der Lieder*) have made him second to Goethe in popularity among composers.

p. 72   'From my great woes': *Aus meinen grossen Schmerzen* ♪ Wolf, 1878.

p. 72   'A fellow loves a girl': *Ein Jüngling liebt ein Mädchen* ♪ Schumann, Op. 48.

p. 74   'I do not know the meaning': *Die Lorelei* ♪ Liszt, 1841.

p. 75   'Silent the night': *Der Doppelgänger* ♪ Schubert, D957.

p. 75   'You are like a flower': *Du bist wie eine Blume* ♪ Liszt, c.1840; Schumann, Op. 25; Wolf, 1876.

p. 76   'A Girl's First Love Song', with its pre-Freudian symbolism, recalls *Popular Rhymes of Scotland* (ed. R. Chambers, 1858), which gives under the heading of Marriage: 'Put your hand in the creel,/ And draw an adder or an eel', though Mörike has 'net'. *Erstes Liebeslied eines Mädchens* ♪ Wolf, 1888.

p. 77   'The Forsaken Maid': *Das verlassene Mägdlein* ♪ Schumann, Op. 64; Wolf, 1888.

p. 77   'Fair Rohtraut'. The poet relates how, looking through a dictionary, his eye fell on some forgotten old German girls' names, among them Rohtraut. Knowing her immediately for a princess, he stepped out of his study into the garden, where he 'discovered' the poem. It was translated by Meredith (1851). *Schön-Rohtraut* ♪ Schumann, Op. 67.

p. 79   'Domestic Scene' celebrates the minutiae of married life; cf. Louis MacNeice, 'Les Sylphides'. The schoolmaster's name seems to be a joke: in Classical Latin *ciborium* means 'goblet' (but quite other things in Church Latin). Rike is short for Friederike. The form is the Classical elegiac couplet as used by Goethe (p. 55).

p. 83   Theodor Storm, known mainly as a writer of fiction, wrote some uncomfortably truthful love poems.

p. 85   Groth was a Holsteiner (in Germany's far north) who revived literature in his dialect, which approaches Dutch.

p. 86   C. F. Meyer, the only Swiss poet in this anthology, wrote historical romances, and poems that combine Classical discipline with late Romantic melancholy.

p. 88   'Two People' (*Zwei Menschen*) is a verse novel whose opening section, translated here, inspired Schoenberg's string sextet *Verklärte Nacht* ('Transfigured Night'), Op. 4. According to Malcolm MacDonald's book on Schoenberg (1976), the music is a commentary on the five paragraphs of this section.

p. 88   'this blessed state': German has a similar euphemism (*gesegnet*).

p. 90   'If I do not touch you today': *Wenn ich heut nicht deinen leib berühre* ♪ Schoenberg, Op. 15.

p. 90   'You pure and slender': in later life George envisioned a Spartan-style 'New Realm' (*Reich*) of noble young men, till the realities of the Third Reich drove him into exile.

p. 92   Morgenstern, also known in his day as a mystical writer, is remembered for his nonsense – and not quite nonsense – verse. Here he tells of three bell sounds in a love triangle, and of two parallel lines like the 'loves' in Marvell's poem, which 'though infinite can never meet'.

p. 94   'The Two of Them': *Die Beiden* ♪ Schoenberg, 1899.

p. 95   'Leda' has little in common with Yeats's later sonnet on the same theme. Rilke's sonnet is hardly about Leda at all, but about a man's sexual initiation.

p. 97   Heym, both as prose writer and as poet, anticipates Expressionism, whose heyday he did not live to see.

p. 99   Schwitters, an artist in many media, called his work *Merz*, after a scrap of paper torn from an advertisement for a *Commerz- und Privatbank* in one of his collages. His expulsion from the Dada movement was largely due to his widely popular poem *An* ('To') *Anna Blume*, which is a collage of scraps of talk: it was considered too sympathetic to the banalities it was supposed to be mocking. Here, with its echo of Chamisso ('you most glorious of all', cf. p. 66), is that first *Merz*-poem in what can only be called the author's own *Merz*-translation. Anna Blume becomes 'eve Blossom'; in German she *hat ein Vogel*, she (literally) has a bird, she is cuckoo, but in *Merz*-English she has wheels . . .

p. 101 'Ode to Joy': Kästner's contribution to a centenary commemoration of Beethoven's death (1927) cost him his job on a Dresden newspaper. The translation attempts to match the puns throughout, but the delicious penultimate line, *Nun senkst du deine Lider ohne Worte* ('Now you lower your eyelids/*Lieder*, songs without words'), echoing Mendelssohn, resisted all matchmaking.

p. 102 'Pihi': apparently *pixi* (*x* is palatal *s*), the little grebe; but this has two wings and is not gregarious. More likely is the mythical one-winged *biyi*. Birds are often invoked in Chinese poetry as models of marital fidelity.

p. 103 'pain through friction': the Centaurs have arrived.

INDEX OF POETS

Anonymous	11–13	Hofmann von Hofmannswaldau,	
Brentano, Clemens	64	Christian	34
Chamisso, Adelbert von	66	Hölderlin, Friedrich	61–3
Dehmel, Richard	88–9	Jandl, Ernst	103
Der von Kürenberc	14	Kaléko, Mascha	102
Des Knaben Wunderhorn	65	Kästner, Erich	101
Droste-Hülshoff, Annette von	70–1	Meyer, Conrad Ferdinand	86–7
Eichendorff, Joseph von	67	Morgenstern, Christian	92–3
Fleming, Paul	32	Mörike, Eduard	76–82
George, Stefan	90–1	Müller, Wilhelm	68
Gleim, Johann Wilhelm		Opitz, Martin	30–1
Ludwig	40	Platen, August von	69
Goethe, Johann Wolfgang von	41–58	Rilke, Rainer Maria	95–6
Gottfried von Strassburg	24–6	Schwitters, Kurt	99–100
Groth, Klaus	85	Stolle, Gottlieb	36
Gryphius, Andreas	33	Storm, Theodor	83–4
Günther, Johann Christian	37–9	Traditional	27
Heine, Heinrich	72–5	Walther von der Vogelweide	22–3
Heinrich von Morungen	17–19	Weckherlin, Georg Rudolf	29
Henric van Veldeke	15–16	Willemer, Marianne von	59–60
Heym, Georg	97–98	Wolfram von Eschenbach	20–1
Hofmannsthal, Hugo von	94	Zesen, Philipp von	35